A Touch of Whimsey...

Twelve Decorative Pillows for all Occasions
By Abbey Lane Quilts

Table of Contents

Abbey Lane Quilts
www.abbeylanequilts.com
177 E. Magnolia St. Oviedo, FL 32765
© 2011 All Rights Reserved   Abbey Lane Quilts
ISBN 978-0-9828069-2-0

RUFFLES AND ROSES
14" x 14"

MATERIALS

1 yard fabric for pillow
1/2 yard fabric for flowers
14" x 14" pillow form
Fabric Glue

CUTTING INSTRUCTIONS

<u>Pillow</u>
Cut (2) - 6" x WOF for Ruffle Sections
Cut (1) - 4 1/2" x 15" for Center Band
Cut (1) - 15" x 15" for Pillow Back

<u>Flowers</u>
Tear (9) - 1 1/2" x WOF (do not cut - tear fabric)
Cut (3) - 3" circle for flower backs

SEWING INSTRUCTIONS

<u>Pillow</u>
1. Sew a gathering stitch 1/4" from the edge along one of the long sides of each Ruffle Section. Pull the gathering stitches in until it measures 15".

2. With right sides together, pin each gathered edge to the Center Band. Adjust the gathers evenly and sew together with a 1/4" seam. Press seams.

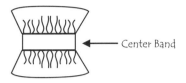

Center Band

3. Sew a gathering stitch 1/2" from the edge on the remaining side of each ruffle section. Pull the gathering stitches in until it measures 15".

4. With right sides together, pin each gathered edge to the Pillow Back. Adjust the gathers evenly. Pin the remaining sides of the pillow front to the back.

5. Sew the front and back together with a 1/2" seam. Be sure to leave a 10" opening in the center of **one side** to put a pillow form in.

6. Turn right side out and insert a pillow form. Stitch the opening closed.

<u>Roses</u>

1. Sew the (3) strips together end to end to form one long strip. Press seams.

2. With wrong sides together, fold the long strip in half lengthwise. Press fold.

3. Tie (2) knots on top of each other on one end. Trim off any excess strip close to the knots.

Tie 2 knots in one end

4. With the folded side of the strip up, **wrap** around the knot once.

5. Now the **twist** - twist the fabric so the raw edge is up and the folded edge is down.

6. Hold the flower between your thumb and fore-finger and use the opposite hand to **wrap** and **twist** as it gets larger to help keep it flat.

Twist and Wrap

7. Keep **wrapping** and **twisting** the fabric around the initial knot.

8. As the rose gets larger you will need to **twist** the fabric more often. Secure the twists and wraps with a little bit of fabric glue. Continue **twisting** and **wrapping** the fabric until the entire fabric strip is used.

9. **Twist** the loose end into the back of the rose and secure with fabric glue. Glue the rose to the flower backing.

10. Repeat steps 1-9 to make 2 more roses.

11. Sew the back of the finished Roses to the Center Section of the pillow.

BLOCK PARTY
18" x 18"

MATERIALS

5 Coordinating Fat Quarters
1/8 yard for Gathered Strips
1/2 yard for Cording Covering
19" x 19" piece for Pillow Back
2 1/4 yards Cording
18" x 18" Pillow Form

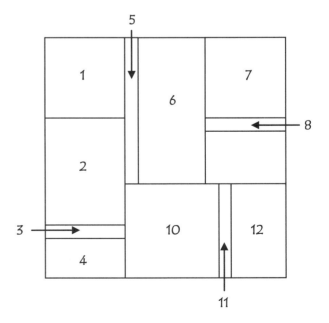

CUTTING INSTRUCTIONS

<u>Fabric 1</u>
Cut (1) – 7" x 7" for Block 1
Cut (1) – 7" x 4 1/2" for Block 9

<u>Fabric 2</u>
Cut (1) – 7" x 8 1/2" for Block 2
Cut (1) – 7" x 7" for Block 7

<u>Fabric 3</u>
Cut (1) – 7" x 4" for Block 4
Cut (1) – 5" x 8" for Block 12

<u>Fabric 4</u>
Cut (1) – 5 1/2" x 12" for Block 6

<u>Fabric 5</u>
Cut (1) – 7 1/2" x 8" for Block 10

<u>Gathering Strips</u>
Cut (2) – 1 1/2" x 14" for Block 3 and 8
Cut (1) – 1 1/2" x 24" for Block 5
Cut (1) – 1 1/2" x 16" for Block 11

<u>Cording Covering</u>
Cut (4) – 4" x WOF

SEWING INSTRUCTIONS

Section 1

1. Sew a gathering stitch 1/4" from the edge along both sides of each of the Gathering Strips Blocks (blocks 3, 5, 8 and 11).

2. Sew Block 1 to Block 2. Press seam.

3. Pull in the gathering stitches on Block 3 until it measures 7". Adjust the gathers evenly and pin to the bottom of Block 2. Sew the blocks together. Press seam.

4. Pin Block 4 to the bottom of Block 3. Sew the blocks together. Press seam.

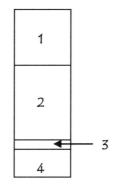

Section 2

5. Pull in the gathering stitches on Block 5 until it measures 12". Adjust the gathers evenly and pin to Block 6. Sew the blocks together. Press seam.

6. Pull in the gathering stitches on Block 8 until it measures 7". Adjust the gathers evenly and pin to the bottom of Block 7. Sew the blocks together. Press seam.

7. Pin Block 9 to the bottom of Block 8. Sew the blocks together. Press seam.

8. Pin Blocks 5 and 6 to Blocks 7, 8 and 9. Sew the blocks together. Press seam.

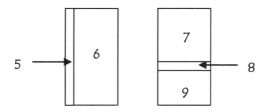

Section 3

9. Pull in the gathering stitches on Block 11 until it measures 8". Adjust the gathers evenly and pin to Block 10. Sew the blocks together. Press seam.

10. Pin Block 12 to Block 11. Sew the blocks together. Press seam.

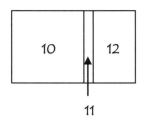

11. Sew Section 2 to Section 3. Press seam. Sew these sections to Section 1. Press seam.

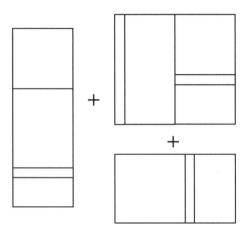

Cording

1. Sew the 4 Cording Covering strips together end to end to form one long piece. Press the seams open.

2. Cut the Cording to 74".

3. With the wrong side up, lay the cording in the center of the Cording Covering piece. Be sure one end of the Cording extends about 2" from the start of the covering piece.

4. Fold the fabric over the cording so the raw edges are even and the right side of the fabric is showing. Sew down the fabric 1/2" from the raw edge. Sew all the way to the end of the fabric, continue sewing even after the cording ends.

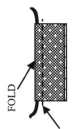

RAW EDGES EVEN   FOLD   STITCH 1/2" FROM THE EDGE

5. Gather in the fabric on the covering until 2" of the cording shows on both ends. Adjust the gathers evenly over the cording. Pin the fabric in place temporarily.

6. Start in the center of the bottom, and start pinning the covered cording to the right side of the pillow top. Be sure the raw edges are even. As you come to each corner, make 3 small clips in the cording seam allowance to allow the cording to curve smoothly around each corner. Be careful when clipping that you don't cut through the stitching line. Cut the ends of the cording so they touch but do not overlap.

7. Unpin the cording and sew the ends of the cording together. Turn a 1/4" under on each end of the fabric and stitch the ends together.

8. Adjust the gathers evenly and repin to the pillow top. Sew the cording in place following the seam line on the cording.

Pillow Assembly

1. With right sides together, pin the Pillow Front to the Pillow Back.

2. Sew the 2 pieces together with a 1/2" seam. Leave a 15" opening in the middle of one side for turning and stuffing.

3. Turn the pillow right side out and stuff with an 18" x 18" pillow form. Sew the opening closed.

PEEK-A-BOO
14" X 20"

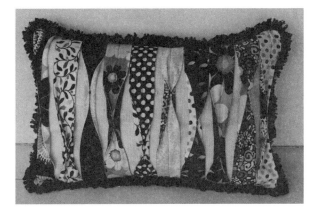

MATERIALS

1/2 yard for Pillow Front (we used Burlap)
1/2 yard for Pillow Back
5 Dark Fabric pieces (2 1/2" x WOF) for Stripes
5 Light Fabric pieces (2 1/2" x WOF) for Stripes
2 yards Trim (optional)
2 Buttons for Pillow Back
Embroidery Floss
14" x 20" Pillow Form

CUTTING INSTRUCTIONS

Pillow Front
Cut (1) – 14 1/2" x 20 1/2"

Pillow Back
Cut (1) – 14 1/2" x 11 1/4" – Top piece
Cut (1) – 14 1/2" x 12 1/4" – Bottom piece

Stripes
Cut (10) – 14 1/2" x 2 1/2" (Dark Fabrics)
Cut (10) – 14 1/2" x 2 1/2" (Light Fabrics)

SEWING INSTRUCTIONS

Pillow Front

1. With right sides together, pin 1 dark stripe to 1 light stripe. Sew a 1/4" seam down each long side of the stripe. Turn right side out and press seams. Repeat these steps to make 9 more stripes.

2. With chalk or an erasable marker, draw a line lengthwise down the center of each stripe. Start a 1/4" from each edge and position the stripes on top of the Pillow Front, alternating the light and dark stripes. Pin the stripes in place.

1/4" in from each edge

3. Sew the stripes in place along the drawn lines. After the stripes are all sewn, sew a 1/4" seam across the top and bottom of the pillow front to hold the ends of each of the stripes in place.

4. If you are using trim, pin it to the pillow front and sew it on with a 1/4" seam.

Pillow Back

1. Fold over a 1/4" along one long side of the Top Back piece and press. Sew a 1/8" top stitch along the fold.

2. Fold over a 1/4" along one long side of the Bottom Back piece and press. Fold that same side over another 1" and press again. Sew a 1/8" top stitch along the fold. Sew an additional top stitch 3/4" from the folded edge.

3. With right sides together, pin the Bottom Back piece to the left side of the Pillow Front. The folded edge will be near the center of the Pillow Front.

4. With right sides together, pin the Top Back piece to the right side of the Pillow Front. The folded edge will be on top of the Bottom Back piece.

5. Sew the 2 back pieces to the Pillow Front with a 1/4" seam around the entire pillow. Turn right side out.

6. Insert a pillow form. Secure the 2 back pieces with a tacking stitch 4 1/2" from each side. Sew a button on top of the tacking stitches.

Finishing Touches

1. Measure down 7" from the **top** of the first strip on the pillow form. Bring the two edges of the stripe into the center line and stitch together with embroidery floss. The back side of the stripe will show.

2. On the second stripe, measure up 5" from the **bottom** and gather in the edges of the stripe. Secure with embroidery floss.

3. On the third stripe, measure down 5" from the **top** and gather in the edges of the stripe and secure.

4. Continue gathering in each of the stripes according to the chart below.

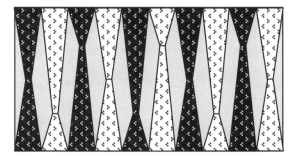

LOLLIPOPS
14" X 28"

MATERIALS

1/2 yard for Background
1/2 yard for Pillow Back
1/2 yard for Ruffle
5 Assorted pieces 2 1/2" x WOF for Flowers
5 Assorted pieces 2" x 12" for Sticks
8 Assorted pieces 16" Ric Rac
14 Assorted Buttons
14" x 28" Pillow Form

CUTTING INSTRUCTIONS

<u>Pillow Background</u>
Cut (1) – 15" x 29"
Cut (5) – 5" x 5" for Flower Bases

<u>Pillow Back</u>
Cut (1) – 15" x 29"

<u>Ruffle</u>
Cut (2) – 9" x WOF

<u>Flowers</u>
Tear (5) strips – 1 1/2" x WOF (both sides of strip need to be torn)

<u>Sticks</u>
Tear (5) strips – 1/2" x 12" (both side of strip need to be torn)

<u>Ric Rac</u>
Cut (8) – 16"

SEWING INSTRUCTIONS

<u>Pillow Front</u>

1. Sew a very loose gathering stitch through the center of a Flower strip. This will naturally gather the strip in about 3-4 inches.

2. Start in the middle of the Flower Base and sew the long strip down to the center. Keep sewing and turning the strip as you wind your way outward. Overlap each row slightly as you go. When you get to the end of the strip secure it with a backstitch. The flower should be approximately 4" when finished.

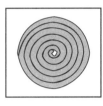

3. Repeat steps 1-2 to make 2 more Large Flowers.

4. To make the small flowers, cut off 9" from the strip before you begin and then follow steps 1-2 to make 2 small flowers. The flowers should be approximately 3" when finished.

5. Trim the Flower base close to the outside stitching line so you can't see it from the front of the flower.

6. Place the flowers on the Pillow Background varying the heights. Pin in place.

7. Tuck each Stick under the flower about 1". Pin and sew in place. We used a Zig Zag stitch down the middle of each stick. The sides are not sewn down so the raw edges will fray. Trim the ends of the sticks even with the Pillow Background.

8. Sew the Flowers in place by stitching over the outside sewing line on each flower.

9. Arrange the Ric Rac and buttons on each side of the flowers. Sew in place.

Pillow Assembly

1. With right sides together, fold a ruffle piece in half lengthwise. Sew each of the short ends together with a 1/4" seam. Turn right side out and press.

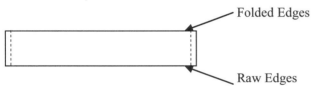

Folded Edges

Raw Edges

2. Sew a gathering stitch along the raw edges. Pull the gathers in to measure 14".

3. With the raw edges even, center the Ruffle on one end of the Pillow Background and pin in place. The ruffle will be 1/2" shorter on each side than the background piece. Sew in place.

4. Repeat steps 1-3 to sew the remaining ruffle to the other end of the pillow background.

5. With right sides together, pin the Pillow Background to the pillow back. Sew together with a 1/2" seam. Leave a 12" opening in the center of the long bottom side for turning and stuffing. Be careful to not sew the Ruffle in the seam.

6. Turn right side out and insert a pillow form. Sew the opening closed.

CONFETTI
20" x 20"

MATERIALS

2/3 yard for Pillow Front
2/3 yard for Pillow Back
1/8 yard for Cording Covering
17 - Assorted Fabric Scraps (5 1/2" x 5 1/2") for Circles
2 yards 12/32" Cording
Poly-fil stuffing
Template Plastic or Cardboard
20" x 20" Pillow Form

CUTTING INSTRUCTIONS

Pillow Front
Cut (1) – 21" x 21"

Pillow Back
Cut (1) – 21" x 21"

Cording Covering
Cut (2) – 2" x WOF

Circles
Cut (1) – Large, Medium and Small Circle templates from Template Plastic or Cardboard
Trace templates on the wrong side of the fabric
Cut out the fabric 1" bigger than the traced circles
Cut (5) – Large Circle Templates
Cut (7) – Medium Circle Templates
Cut (5) – Small Circle Templates

SEWING INSTRUCTIONS

Circles

1. Sew a gathering stitch by hand, around the outside edge of (1) Large fabric circle. Center the Large Circle template on the wrong side of the fabric circle.

2. Pull the gathering stitches in tight and iron the circle. Release the gathers a little bit and remove the template. Pull the gathers back, tie off the gathers and iron the circle again.

3. Repeat steps 1-2 to make the remainder of the circles.

4. With right sides up, place the circles on the Pillow Front. The diagram below is how we placed the circles.

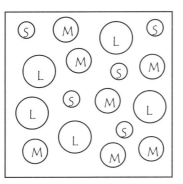

5. Sew the circles to the Pillow Front with a 1/8" top stitch. Leave a 2" opening in the circle and insert enough stuffing to make the circle pop up. Finish sewing the entire way around the circle. Repeat for all the circles.

6. Sew a second top stitch 1/4" from the edge around each circle to give them a more finished look.

Cording

1. Sew the (2) Cording Covering pieces together along the short ends to form one long piece.

2. With the wrong side up, lay the cording in the center of the Cording Covering piece. Fold the covering over the cording so the raw edges are even and the right side of the fabric is showing.

3. Stitch as close as possible to the cording.

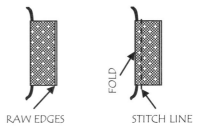

RAW EDGES   STITCH LINE

4. Start in the center the bottom side. Leave about an 1/2" tail and start pinning the covered cording to the right side of the pillow top. Be sure the raw edges are even. As you come to each corner, make 3 small clips in the cording seam allowance to allow the cording to curve smoothly around each corner. Be careful when clipping that you don't cut through the stitching line. Overlap the ends of the cording by 1/2".

Ends of Cording

5. Sew the cording in place following the seam line on the cording covering.

Pillow Assembly

1. With right sides together, pin the Pillow Front to the Pillow Back.

2. Sew the 2 pieces together with a 1/2" seam. Leave a 15" opening in the middle of the bottom side for turning and stuffing.

3. Turn the pillow right side out and stuff with an 20" x 20" pillow form. Sew the opening closed.

IT TAKES TWO
14″ x 18″

MATERIALS

1/4 yard Red Fabric for Pillow Front
1/4 yard White Fabric for Pillow Front
1/3 yard for Heart Backing
1 Fat Quarter for Pillow Back
2 yards – 1/2″ Cording
14″ x 18″ Pillow Form
Assorted embellishments

CUTTING INSTRUCTIONS

Red Fabric
Cut (1) – 7 3/4″ x 19″ for Heart Background
Cut (1) – 6″ x 14″ for Heart

White Fabric
Cut (1) – 7 3/4″ x 19″ for Heart Background
Cut (1) – 6″ x 14″ for Heart

Heart Backing
Cut (1) – 12″ x 14″

Pillow Back
Cut (1) – 15″ x 19″

SEWING INSTRUCTIONS

Pillow Front

1. Sew the Red and White Heart pieces together lengthwise with a 1/4″ seam. Press seam. This will be the Heart Front.

2. Center the Heart Template on the back side of the sewn pieces. Be sure the center line on the template matches up with the seam line. Trace around the template with chalk or an erasable marker. This will be your sewing line.

3. With right sides together, pin the Heart Front to the Heart Backing. Sew the two pieces together along the traced heart outline. Trim around the stitching line leaving a 1/8″ seam allowance.

4. Make a slit in the backing fabric and turn the heart right side out. Press flat.

5. Sew the Red and White Pillow Background pieces together lengthwise with a 1/4″ seam. Press seam.

6. With right sides up, center the Heart on the Pillow Background. The white side of the heart should be on the red side of the background and the red side of the heart should be on the white side of the background. Pin the heart in place. Sew the heart to the background with a 1/8″ top stitch.

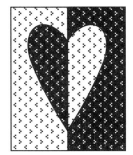

Cording

1. Start in the center of the bottom and pin the cording to the pillow front. Be sure to line up the cording so the seam will be 1/2″ from the outer edge of the pillow. Leave a 1″ tail on the cording at the beginning and at the end.

2. Sew the cording to the pillow front with a 1/2″ seam. Trim the ends of the cording to 1/2″.

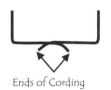

Ends of Cording

Pillow Assembly

1. With right sides together, pin the Pillow Back to the Pillow Front.

2. Sew the two pieces together with a 1/2″ seam. Leave a 12″ opening in the middle of the bottom side for turning and stuffing.

3. Turn the pillow right side out and stuff with a 14″ x 18″ pillow form. Sew the opening closed

Embellishments

1. Attach ribbon and berries to the center of the Heart.

LIBERTY
16″ x 16″

MATERIALS

6 Coordinating Fabric pieces (5″ x 14″) for Pillow Top
1 Light piece (8 1/2″ x 8 1/2″) for Center Section
1 Contrasting Piece (8″ x 8″) for Star
1/2 yard for Pillow Back
16″ x 16″ Pillow Form

CUTTING INSTRUCTIONS

Center Section
Cut (1) - 8 1/2″ x 8 1/2″

Star
Cut (1) - Star Template

Pillow Backing
Cut (1) - 16 1/2″ x 9 1/2″ for Bottom piece
Cut (1) - 16 1/2″ x 10 1/2″ for Top piece

SEWING INSTRUCTIONS

Pillow Front

1. With the right side up, layer the 6 Coordinating Fabrics on top of each other.

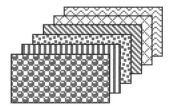

It Takes
Two

Confetti

Spooky

Bewitched

Evergreen

Christmas Joy

Liberty

Frosty

2. Cut the stack into 8 smaller angled pieces. Place your ruler at an angle and cut. There is no right or wrong way to do this. Just try to vary the angles of the lines so you get some different shapes.

HINT – If you are nervous about cutting, make some sample lines with chalk to get the size and angle you like before cutting.

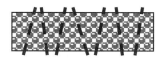

CUTTING LINES

3. Now the fun part – MIXING it all up. Separate each of your cuts just a little. Leave the 1st stack alone.

4. Take the top piece from the 2nd stack and place it on the bottom of the stack.

5. Take the top 2 pieces from the 3rd stack and place them on the bottom of the stack.

6. Take the top 3 pieces from the 4th stack and place them on the bottom of the stack.

7. Continue mixing up the pieces with the remaining stacks until they have all been mixed up. No stacks that are side by side should have the same fabric showing.

8. Start with the first piece and sew the top piece of each stack together in order one at a time. Press all the seams in the same direction. Continue sewing the pieces together until you have 6 strips.

9. Trim each strip to 4 1/2″ wide.

10. Sew 1 strip to each side of the Center Section. Trim the strip even with the Center Section.

11. Sew 2 strips together. Sew this longer strip to the top of the Center Section. Trim even.

12. Sew the remaining 2 strips together. Sew this strip to the bottom of the Center Section. Trim even.

13. Center the Star in the Center Section. Sew in place with your favorite appliqué method. We used a Blanket Stitch.

Pillow Backing

1. Fold over a 1/4″ along one long side of the Bottom Back piece and press. Sew a 1/8″ top stitch along the fold.

2. Fold over a 1/4″ along one long side of the Top Back piece and press. Fold that same side over another 1″ and press again. Sew a 1/8″ top stitch along the fold. Sew an additional top stitch 3/4″ from the folded edge.

3. With right sides together, pin the Bottom Back piece to the bottom of the Pillow Front. The folded edge will be near the center of the Pillow Front.

4. With right sides together, pin the Top Back piece to the top of the Pillow Front. The folded edge will be on top of the Bottom Back piece.

5. Sew the 2 back pieces to the Pillow Front with a 1/4″ seam around the entire pillow. Turn right side out.

6. Insert a pillow form. Secure the 2 back pieces with a tacking stitch in the center of the folded edge. Sew a button on top of the tacking stitches.

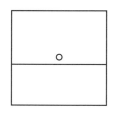

SPOOKY
10" x 16"

MATERIALS

1 Fat Quarter for Pillow Front
1 Fat Quarter for Pillow Back
Fabric Scraps for Letters and eyes
1 3/4 yards - Large Ric Rac
5 yards - 6" Netting
Fusible Webbing
10" x 16" Pillow Form

CUTTING INSTRUCTIONS

Pillow Front
Cut (1) - 11" x 17"

Pillow Back
Cut (1) - 11" x 17"

Letters and Eyes
Reverse Letter and Eye pieces before tracing onto
Fusible Webbing
Iron the traced shape to the wrong side of fabric
scraps
Cut out each shape

SEWING INSTRUCTIONS

1. Position the letters on the Pillow Front.
    Insert the "Inside Eye" underneath the "O"
    letters. The "Eye Pupil" will go on last. Iron
    in place.

2. Sew the letters and eyes with a 1/8" top stitch
    to keep in place.

3. With chalk or an erasable marker, draw a line
    1/2" from the outer edge of the pillow front.
    Center the Ric Rac over the drawn line and
    stitch down the center to attach it to the
    pillow front. Sew a Zig Zag stitch across each
    end of the Ric Rac to prevent it from
    raveling.

4. Fold the netting in half lengthwise and sew a
    gathering stitch 1/2" from the raw edge.
    Gather the netting in until it measures 53".
    Adjust the gathers evenly and pin to the
    front of the pillow front, the ends should
    overlap by 1/2". Stitch in place with a 1/2"
    seam.

5. With right sides together, pin the Pillow
    Front to the Pillow Back. Sew the 2 pieces
    together with a 1/2" seam. Leave a 10"
    opening in the center of the bottom side for
    turning and stuffing.

BEWITCHED

13″ x 17″

MATERIALS

1 Fat Quarter for Pillow Front
1 Fat Quarter for Pillow Back
1 Black Fat Quarter for Hat Base
Assorted Fabric Scraps for Hat and Spider
3/4 yard for Ruffle
2/3 yard Netting for Ruffle
Large, Medium and Small Ric Rac
Fusible Webbing
13″ x 17″ Pillow Form

CUTTING INSTRUCTIONS

Pillow Front
Cut (1) – 14″ x 18″

Pillow Back
Cut (1) – 14″ x 18″

Assorted Scraps
Reverse Hat and Spider pieces and trace onto
Fusible Webbing
Iron the traced shapes to the wrong side of fabric
scraps
Cut out each shape

Ruffle
Tear (4) – 6″ x WOF

Netting
Cut (5) – 5″ x WOF – 4 for the Ruffle and 1 for
the Bow

SEWING INSTRUCTIONS

Hat

1. Arrange the Hat pieces onto the Base Hat
   piece. Iron into place.

2. Stitch a piece of the Small Ric Rac between
   each piece. The Ric Rac should cover the raw
   edges of each piece.

3. Stitch a piece of the Large Ric Rac on the
   seam of the Hat Brim.

Pillow Front

1. Position the pieced Hat onto the Pillow
   Front and iron into place.

2. Trace the Spider Web on the upper left corner
   of the Pillow Front. Trace the Spider Web
   hanging from the hat and the Spider's legs.
   Stitch over the lines either by hand or by

3. Position the Spider onto the Pillow Front and iron into place.

4. Stitch a piece of Medium Ric Rac around the outside of the Hat to cover up the raw edges of each piece.

Ruffle

1. Sew the (4) Ruffle pieces together end to end to make a large circle. Press the seams open. With wrong sides together, fold the ruffle in half lengthwise and press.

2. Sew (4) Netting pieces together end to end to make a large circle. Fold in half lengthwise. The extra piece of Netting will be used for the bow on the hat.

3. With the folded edges even, layer the netting on top of the ruffle. Sew a gathering stitch through both pieces a 1/4" from the folded edge.

4. Gather the circle in to measure 60". Adjust the gathers evenly and pin to the pillow front. The folded edges should be even with the edge of the pillow front. Sew into place with a 1/4" seam.

Pillow Assembly

1. With right sides together, pin the pillow front to the pillow back. Sew the pieces together with a 1/2" seam. Leave a 9" opening in the center of the bottom side for turning and stuffing.

2. Turn the pillow right side out and stuff with a 13" x 17" pillow form. Sew the opening closed.

3. Tie a bow from the remaining Netting piece.

CHRISTMAS JOY
20" x 13"

MATERIALS

1 Fat Quarter for Pillow Front
1 Fat Quarter for Pillow Back
2/3 yard for Ruffle
Assorted Fabric Scraps for Letters, Poinsettia and Holly Leaves
2 yards – 1" Pom Poms
Fusible Webbing
Embellishments – Jingle Bell, Pom Poms, and Netting
20" x 13" Pillow Form

CUTTING INSTRUCTIONS

Pillow Front
Cut (1) – 14" x 21"

Pillow Back
Cut (1) – 14" x 21"

Ruffle
Cut (4) – 6" x WOF

<u>Letters</u>
Reverse Letter pieces before tracing onto Fusible Webbing

Iron the traced shape to the wrong side of fabric scraps

Cut out each shape

<u>Poinsettia</u>
Cut (1) - Large Poinsettia Flower
Cut (1) - Small Poinsettia Flower

<u>Holly Leaves</u>
Cut (4) - Holly Leaf Templates

SEWING INSTRUCTIONS

1. Position the letters on the Pillow Front. Add the top of the "J". Iron in Place.

2. Sew the letters with a 1/8" top stitch to keep in place.

3. Layer the 2 Poinsettia Flowers together. Sew or Glue 6 pearls in the center of the Small Poinsettia Flower.

4. Place the Poinsettia Flowers and Holly Leaves on the letters. Tack into place. (You can glue these pieces in place if you prefer.)

5. Sew the Pom Poms to the right side of the Pillow Front a 1/4" from the outside edge.

6. Sew the (4) Ruffle pieces together end to end to form one large circle. Press seams open.

7. With wrong sides together, fold the ruffle in half lengthwise and press. Sew a gathering stitch 1/4" from the raw edge around the entire circle. With the raw edges even pin the ruffle to the pillow front. The ruffle will be over the Pom Poms. Sew the pieces together with a 1/4" seam.

8. With right sides together, pin the Pillow Front the to Pillow Back. Sew the pieces together with a 1/2" seam. Leave a 14" opening along the bottom side for turning and stuffing.

9. Turn the pillow right side out and stuff with a 20" x 13" pillow form. Sew the opening closed.

10. Add any little extras to the letters. Here are some suggestions:

    Small Jingle Bells to the top of the "J"

    Medium Jingle bell to the tip of the "J"

    Cut a strip of Netting, gather the strip in the center and tack to the Holly Leaves. Add 3 small pom poms.

EVERGREEN
14" Circle

MATERIALS

8 Assorted Green Fat Quarters for leaves
1 White Fat Quarter for Pillow Front
1 Green Fat Quarter for Pillow Back
1/4 yard Red for Bow
2 yards Fusible Webbing

CUTTING INSTRUCTIONS

Green Fabrics for Leaves
Cut into 5" lengths

Pillow Front
Cut (1) - 15" circle for Pillow Front

Pillow Back
Cut (1) - 15" circle for Pillow Back

Red Fabric
Cut (1) - 6 1/2" x WOF for Bow

SEWING INSTRUCTIONS

1. With wrong sides together, fuse 2 green pieces together.

2. Trace leaf template on fused green fabric. Cut out exactly on traced lines. You will need approximately 95 leaves.

3. With right sides up, lay out leaves along the edge of the Pillow Front. The ends of the leaves should extend about 1" over the edge of the circle. Go around the entire circle. Pin into place.

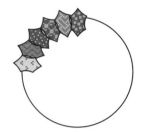

4. Start at the inside tip and stitch down the center of each leaf approximately 2". Sew each leaf to the Pillow Top.

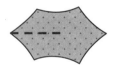

5. Add a second layer of leaves to the pillow top. Come down about 1/2" from the first row and place the leaves in between the first row. Repeat step 4 to sew each leaf down.

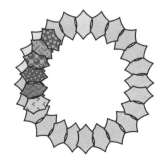

6. Repeat step 5 to add 3 more layers of leaves to the Pillow Front. Leave a 3" circle open in the center so the Pillow Front show through.

Each row of leaves in the diagram is made with a single fabric so you can see the rows clearly. The pillow should be sewn with multiple fabric leaves in each row to add more interest.

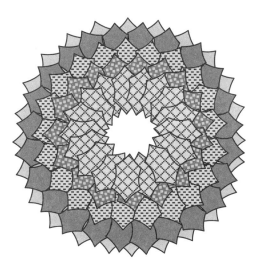

7. With right sides together, pin the Pillow Back to the Pillow Front. Carefully fold down the leaves so the don't get caught in the seam. Sew the two pieces together leaving a 10" opening on the bottom.

8. Turn the pillow right side out and stuff with a 15" pillow form. Sew the opening closed.

Bow

1. With right sides together, fold the Red Fabric in half lengthwise and press. Sew down the long side with a 1/4". Turn right side out and press.

2. Tie a bow. Fold in a 1/4" on each end and sew shut.

3. Tack the bow to the wreath.

FROSTY
15" x 18"

MATERIALS

3 Coordinating Fat Quarters for Pillow Front
1 Fat Quarter - for Pillow Backing
White wool for Snowman
Black wool for Hat and Boots
Gold wool for Mittens and Stars
Orange wool for Nose
Plaid wool for Scarf
Embellishments
Tan Rit Dye

CUTTING INSTRUCTIONS

Coordinating Fat Quarters
Cut (5) - 1 1/2" x 22" from each fat quarter for Blocks

Wool
If you want an old vintage look, dip the wool pieces in Rit Tan dye. The longer you leave it in the dye, the darker it gets.
White Wool - cut Snowman head and body
Black Wool - cut Hat Top, Hat Brim, Right Boot and Left Boot
Gold Wool - cut Right Mitten, Left Mitten, Large Star and Small Star
Orange Wool - cut Nose
Plaid Wool - cut 3/4" x 14" for Scarf

SEWING INSTRUCTIONS

Blocks

1. Sew 1 strip from each fat quarter together. Press seams. Make 6 more sets.

2. Cut each set into (6) 3 1/2" blocks. There should be 30 blocks total.

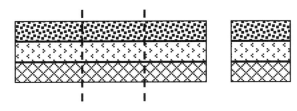

3. Lay out 5 blocks to make a row. Turn every other block sideways so the following pattern is achieved. Lay out 6 rows. Sew each row together with a 1/4" seam. Press the seams in the directions of the arrows. Sew the 6 rows together with a 1/4" seam.

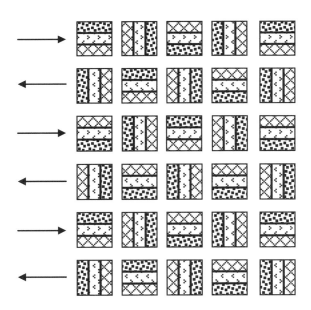

Pillow Assembly

1. Fold the right side over to the wrong side 1" on each side of the Pillow back and press.

2. With wrong sides together, lay the Pillow Front on top of the Pillow Back. Bring the folded edges over the Pillow Front.

3. Sew the 2 pieces together a 1/4" from the folded edge of the pillow. Sew around the entire pillow, do not leave an opening.

4. Make a cut in the excess fabric from the pillow back every 3/8" around the entire pillow. After you have clipped the entire pillow, throw it in the washer and dryer. This will allow the clipped edges to fray.

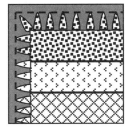

HINT - If you want an old vintage look, soak the pillow in Rit Tan dye **before** you wash and dry it.

5. After the Pillow has been washed and dried. Open the seam along the bottom side and insert the pillow form. Sew the pillow back shut.

Snowman

1. Lay out the Snowman on the Pillow Front. Sew the pieces on with your favorite appliqué stitch.

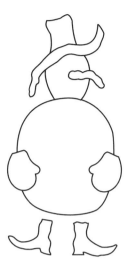

2. Sew on eyes with Black embroidery thread. We used a stick for the mouth but you can use black thread also. Tie a knot in the scarf and attach to the neck, tack the ends over each of the mittens.

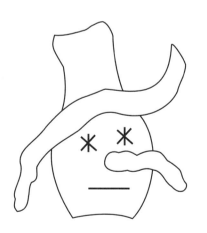

3. Add any additional embellishments. We used small Jingle Bells for buttons and Medium Jingle Bells in each corner of the pillow. We also used sticks for the legs and to hold up the stars.

Pillow Form Basics

It's easy to find ready made pillow forms, but sometimes you need a size that's not available. In that case you can make your own

Follow these easy steps to make your own.

1. Find the size of pillow form you need. For example 12" x 18".

2. Add an inch to each measurement, which will give you 13" x 19".

3. Cut 2 pieces of fabric 13" x 19". We used inexpensive Muslin for our pillow forms.

4. With right sides together, sew the 2 pieces with a 1/2" seam. Leave an opening on the bottom side of turning and stuffing.

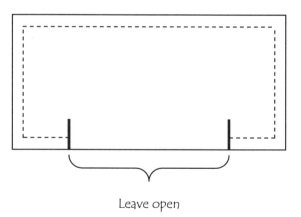

Leave open

5. turn right side out and fill with stuffing. We used Poly-fil - polyester fiberfill.

The advantage of making your own pillow form is that you can make it as full or as flat as you like.

6. Stitch the opening closed.

Bewitched - Spider Web
and Spider

Christmas Joy - Small and
Large Poinsettias

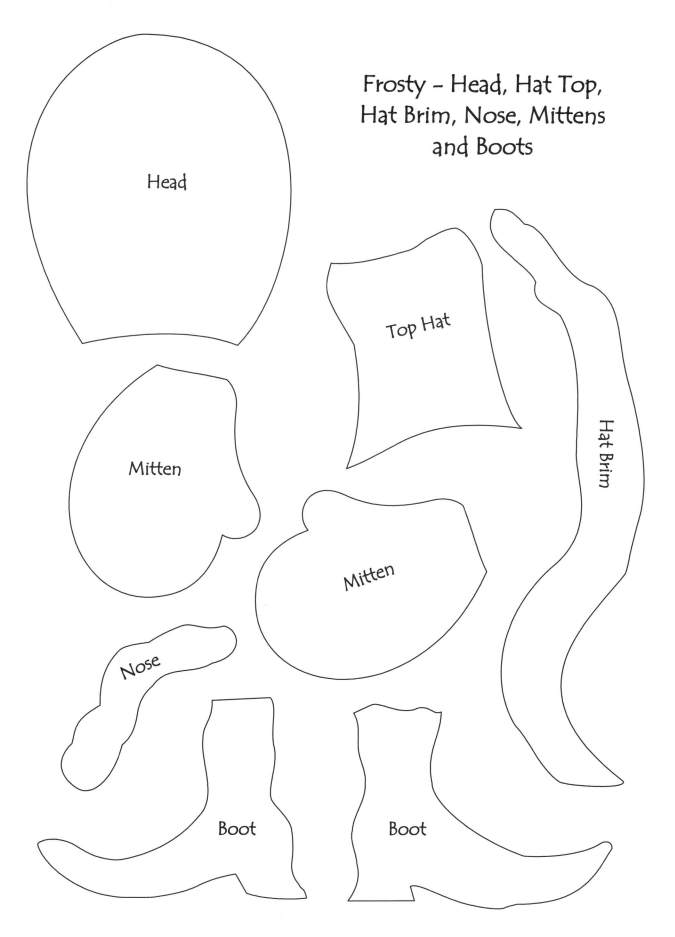

Frosty – Head, Hat Top, Hat Brim, Nose, Mittens and Boots

Head

Top Hat

Hat Brim

Mitten

Mitten

Nose

Boot

Boot

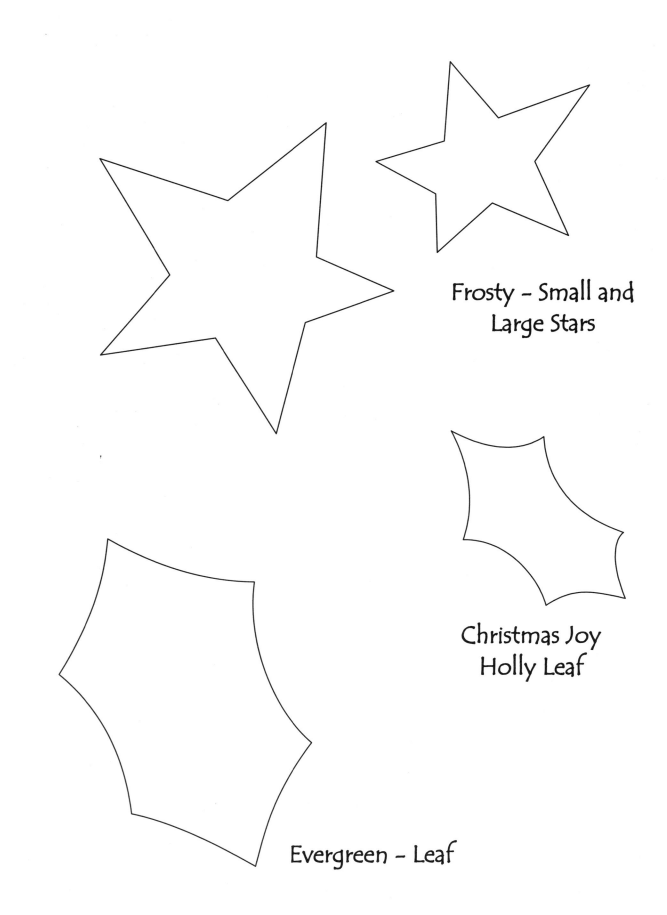

Frosty – Small and
Large Stars

Christmas Joy
Holly Leaf

Evergreen – Leaf